Camels
close their noses
desert animals

By MARK OBLINGER

Illustrated by RYAN WHEATCROFT

CANTATA
LEARNING
MANKATO, MINNESOTA

WWW.CANTATALEARNING.COM

CANTATA LEARNING

MANKATO, MINNESOTA

Published by Cantata Learning
1710 Roe Crest Drive
North Mankato, MN 56003
www.cantatalearning.com

Library of Congress Control Number: 2014956897
978-1-63290-252-8 (hardcover/CD)
978-1-63290-404-1 (paperback/CD)
978-1-63290-446-1 (paperback)

Camels Close Their Noses: Desert Animals by Mark Oblinger
Illustrated by Ryan Wheatcroft

Book design, Tim Palin Creative
Editorial direction, Flat Sole Studio
Executive musical production and direction, Elizabeth Draper
Music arranged and produced by Mark Oblinger

Printed in the United States of America.

VISIT
WWW.CANTATALEARNING.COM/ACCESS-OUR-MUSIC
TO SING ALONG TO THE SONG

Deserts are dry areas that get very little **precipitation**.
Some will go years without a drop of rain! Many deserts
are also very hot. Animals in these places mostly come
out at night, when the sun has set and it's cooler.

Now turn the page, and sing along.

Leave out an *s* in "dessert,"
and instead of a cake,

you will have a "desert,"
which is a very dry place.

Camels close their noses
to keep out sand and dust.

They have a hump or two,

which **provides** a spare lunch.

Rattlesnakes shake their tails
to warn everyone away.

Some snakes blend in with the sand
to hide and wait for **prey**.

Leave out an *s* in "dessert,"
and instead of a cake,

you will have a "desert,"
which is a very dry place.

Roadrunners don't need to fly
when they are hungry.

They run after lizards and snakes,
hunting at top speed.

A desert tortoise hides in its shell
instead of running away.

And it will **burrow** underground
on hot desert days.

17

Meerkats stand on guard
around their **colony**.

Each member works together
to **protect** their families.

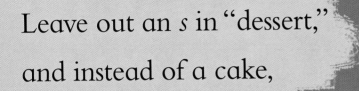

Leave out an *s* in "dessert,"
and instead of a cake,

you will have a "desert,"
which is a very dry place.

SONG LYRICS
Camels Close Their Noses: Desert Animals

Leave out an s in "dessert,"
and instead of a cake,
you will have a "desert,"
which is a very dry place.

Camels close their noses
to keep out sand and dust.

They have a hump or two,
which provides a spare lunch.

Rattlesnakes shake their tails
to warn everyone away.

Some snakes blend in with the sand
to hide and wait for prey.

Leave out an s in "dessert,"
and instead of a cake,
you will have a "desert,"
which is a very dry place.

Roadrunners don't need to fly
when they are hungry.

They run after lizards and snakes,
hunting at top speed.

A desert tortoise hides in its shell
instead of running away.

And it will burrow underground
on hot desert days.

Meerkats stand on guard
around their colony.

Each member works together
to protect their families.

Leave out an s in "dessert,"
and instead of a cake,
you will have a "desert,"
which is a very dry place.

Camels Close Their Noses: Desert Animals

Spaghetti Western
Mark Oblinger

Chorus

Leave out an *s* in "des-sert," and in-stead of a cake, you will have a "de-sert," which is a ver-y dry place.

Verse

1. Cam-els close their nos - es to keep out sand and dust. They have a hump or two, which pro-vides a spare lunch.

Verse 2

Rattlesnakes shake their tails
to warn everyone away.
Some snakes blend in with the sand
to hide and wait for prey.

Verse 3

Roadrunners don't need to fly
when they are hungry.
They run after lizards and snakes,
hunting at top speed.

Verse 4

A desert tortoise hides in its shell
instead of running away.
And it will burrow underground
on hot desert days.

Chorus

Bridge

Meer-kats stand on guard. a - round their col-o - ny. Each mem-ber works to-geth-er to pro-tect their fam-i-lies.

Chorus

GLOSSARY

burrow—to dig

colony—a group of animals living together

on guard—watching for danger

precipitation—rain or snow that falls to the ground

prey—an animal hunted by another animal for food

protect—to keep safe from harm

provides—gives

GUIDED READING ACTIVITIES

1. The title of this story is *Camels Close Their Noses.* Think of other possible titles for this book.

2. Which animals in this book hunt other animals for food? Which are prey?

3. Draw your favorite animal from the book. What features help it survive in the desert?

TO LEARN MORE

Auch, Alison. *Life in the Desert*. Mankato, MN: Capstone, 2012.

Callery, Sean. *Life Cycles: Desert*. London: Kingfisher-Macmillan Children's, 2012.

Kalman, Bobbie. *Baby Animals in Desert Habitats*. New York: Crabtree, 2011.

Murphy, Julie. *Desert Animal Adaptations*. Mankato, MN: Capstone, 2012.